A Great Idea

Home Windmills

by Cherese Cartlidge

NORWOOD HOUSE  PRESS

Norwood House Press
PO Box 316598
Chicago, Illinois 60631

For information regarding Norwood House Press, please visit our Web site at:

www.norwoodhousepress.com or call 866-565-2900.

PHOTO CREDITS: Cover: © Dave Ellison/Alamy; AP Images, 12, 39; © Arco Images GmbH/Alamy, 9; Bow Publications, 6; © Brendan MacNeil/Alamy, 11; Courtesy of Southwest Windpower, 17, 19, 22, 23, 25, 29, 35, 38; © Dave Ellison/Alamy, 32; © David Kadlubowski/Corbis, 15; © George D. Lepp/Corbis, 13; © Joseph Paris, 42; © Jim West, 5; National Geographic/Getty Images, 27; © TWPhoto/Corbis, 41; © Xiaobo Chen/Alamy, 8

Paperback ISBN: 978-1-60357-069-5

The Library of Congress has cataloged the original hardcover edition with the following call number: 2008024190

This paperback edition was published in 2011.

Printed in Heshan City, Guangdong, China.
188P–082011.

Contents

Note: Words that are **bolded** in the text are defined in the glossary on page 43.

Chapter 1

The Many Costs of Electricity

The cost of electricity is rising even with power plants like this one in Michigan working around the clock.

Ellie Dorchincez lives in Benton, Illinois. She worries about the small grocery store she runs there. She had to start closing the store an hour early each day. She also had to shut down one of the large freezers. She did these things to save money on electricity. But she fears she may have to lay off some of the people who work for her. Dorchincez and her grocery store are the victims of rapidly rising power costs. The electric bill for her little grocery store used to be about eight hundred dollars a month. But in 2007 it soared to eighteen hundred dollars per month.

The High Cost of Electricity

In 2007 energy costs in the United States rose 17.4 percent. That kind of jump meant higher bills for everyone.

The average home in the United States uses electric power for many small items. These include small appliances like alarm clocks, lamps, and coffeemakers. It also includes larger items, such as computers and TVs. Many homes also use electric power for heating and cooling.

The cost of electric power varies from state to state. But the average family in

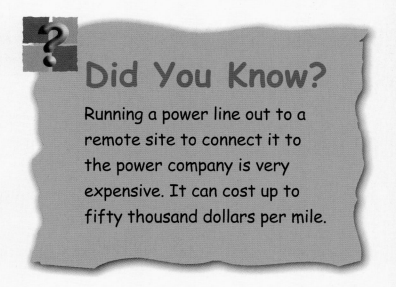

Did You Know?

Running a power line out to a remote site to connect it to the power company is very expensive. It can cost up to fifty thousand dollars per mile.

the United States has been paying about 100 to 150 dollars per month. People in some other countries pay even more. Denmark has had some of the highest power costs in the world. People have paid more than twice as much there as they do in the United States. And the price of electric power continues to go up all over the world.

Fossil Fuels

Why does electricity cost so much? Electric power is mostly generated from the use of **fossil fuels**. Most of the world's electric power comes from coal, oil, and natural gas. These are called fossil fuels because they come from fossils buried under the earth's surface. About two-thirds of the world's electric power comes from burning fossil fuels. That is a huge amount. The reason is that fossil fuels are still the cheapest fuel available. But they will run out some day. And fossil fuels are not the best for our environment.

Burning fossil fuels makes smoke and other air pollution. Air pollution is harmful to plants and

1. All plants take in carbon dioxide from the air.

2. Some prehistoric plants and animals were buried deep in the earth after they died.

3. After millions of years and tons of pressure, the dead plants and animals turned into oil and coal, also called fossil fuels.

4. When fossil fuels are burned, they release carbon dioxide and other greenhouse gases into the air.

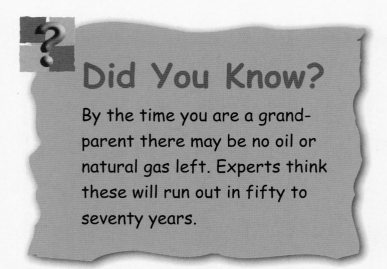

animals. It makes it hard for people to breathe. It can also add to health problems like asthma and bronchitis.

Fossil fuels also emit **carbon dioxide** when they are burned. The level of carbon dioxide in the air rose sharply during the past century. This is because humans have started burning more and more fossil fuels. They have to burn more to make enough power to meet all their needs. Experts think the extra carbon dioxide in the air is trapping too much of the earth's heat. And that is causing a rise in global temperatures. This adds to the problem of **global warming**.

Other Sources of Electricity

What about the other one-third of electrical power? Where does it come from? Roughly half of it comes from nuclear power. Nuclear power does not pollute the air. But the use of nuclear power makes waste materials that are very toxic. Thousands of tons of nuclear waste are stored in the United States alone.

Nuclear waste is dangerous to the health of people and animals. It is also harmful to the planet. It must be disposed of safely.

The Three Gorges Dam

The Three Gorges Dam is in China. It is the biggest hydroelectric river dam in the world. It took 463,000 tons (420,000t) of steel to build the dam. That's enough steel to build thirty-seven hundred copies of the Statue of Liberty! It also took 36.6 million cubic yards (28 million cu. m) of concrete to build the dam. That is enough concrete to build ten Hoover Dams. The power plant at Three Gorges Dam sends power to fifteen provinces in China. This power is used by millions of people.

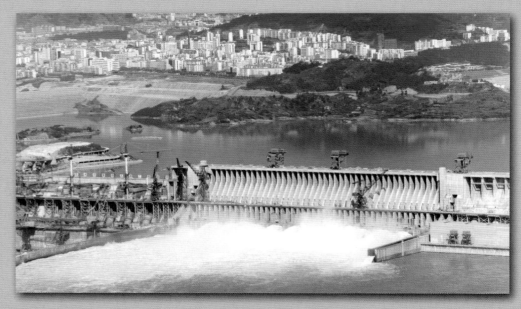

Three Gorges Dam provides electric power to millions of people in China.

Most of it is buried in special containers below ground. But the waste stays poisonous for thousands of years. It is not possible to ensure that disposal sites will still be safe that far into the future. Many countries want to make more nuclear power. But some countries are afraid of using it.

Almost all of the rest of the world's power comes from **hydroelectric dams**. These dams do not pollute the air or make carbon dioxide like fossil fuels do. The main problem with dams is that they need to be built in very specific places. A large body of running water needs to exist. This includes rivers and lakes. Most of the world's major rivers and lakes already have dams on them. That means the world is already getting about all the power from dams that it can.

Different Ways to Make Electricity

People are trying to harvest other natural resources in addition to water to make power. Natural resources do not pollute the air or make poisonous waste. Other sources of power include using the sun for solar power and the wind for wind power.

Windmills have been used for power for centuries. Windmills change wind into

Wind power has been used for hundreds of years. The Netherlands is dotted with old windmills like this one.

Wind-Powered Radios

Windmills used to be a common sight on farms and in rural areas around the world. Their main use was to pump water from wells and to mill grain. By the early twentieth century, people found another use for windmills. At that time radio programs were first being broadcast. Many farmers lived in rural areas that had no electric lines to bring power. So they strung a wire from the windmill to bring power into the house for the radio.

In the 1920s more than a million windmills were used on farms in the United States. Then, in the 1930s power lines were put up in rural areas. This brought power to people all over the country. Now everybody could get power at a very low cost. People in rural areas no longer needed their windmills.

energy. They can be used to **mill** grain or pump water. The earliest windmills were used to mill grain as far back as the seventh century A.D. Modern windmills are used to create electricity.

Today only about 1 percent of the world's power comes from the wind. But some countries get more of their power from wind than others. Denmark gets 20 percent of its power from wind. Germany

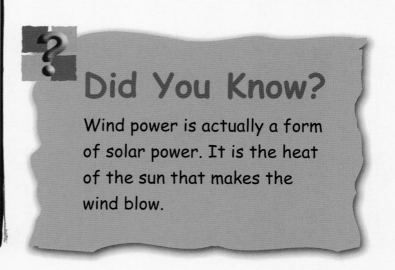

Did You Know?

Wind power is actually a form of solar power. It is the heat of the sun that makes the wind blow.

and Spain both get about 10 percent.

Many countries in the world harvest the wind for energy. They use huge, commercial wind farms. These are built in areas that get a lot of wind. One of the world's most powerful wind farms is in Scotland. It has twenty-four wind **turbines**. Each turbine is 246 feet (75m) high. This wind farm makes enough power for twenty-two thousand homes. That means that just one of these turbines can make enough power for over nine hundred homes.

A wind farm in Scotland is home to giant modern turbines. Wind farms need large tracts of land.

These windmills are much too big to use for your home. Because they are so large, they can only be used in places that have winds strong enough to turn the blades. They also need more land than most homes have. Yet home windmills are

Home Windmills

David Calley's basic idea was not new. Windmills have been around for centuries. A windmill that is used to make electricity is called a wind turbine. But no matter what they are called, windmills work by changing wind into energy. The wind makes the blades of a windmill turn. A shaft is connected to the blades. The turning blades make the shaft spin. This shaft is also hooked up to a generator. The generator changes the energy of the spinning shaft into electricity.

Today's home windmills have blades that look a lot like the propeller of an airplane. The blades are mounted on top of metal poles. These poles are anywhere from 33 to 100 feet (10 to 30m) high. This makes the home windmill look something like an airplane propeller spinning atop a metal telephone pole.

A Texas man inspects his new home windmill. Many people are looking for ways to create their own energy.

A man climbs a home power wind turbine. Windmills have become small enough for ordinary families to use.

possible. In many areas, ordinary families can use windmills to help them make their own power. As power gets more expensive, people do not have to rely on fossil fuels to make their electricity.

In the mid-1980s two young men in Arizona started looking for a way that people could use windmills on their own property. Their names are David Calley and Andy Kruse.

Chapter 2

The Modern Home Windmill Is Born

Like lots of kids, David Calley loved to tinker with machines. But his machines really worked. When he was only twelve years old, he built his first small windmill. He rigged it up so that it ran the lights in his bedroom and his cassette player.

Calley did not stop there. He started building larger windmills that made more power. His friends and neighbors saw how well his windmill worked and wanted one, too. When he was in high school in the early 1980s, he began selling them to his neighbors. They used the windmills to help make power for their homes.

Calley went on to study physics at Northern Arizona University. He had improved his windmills and was able to make them cheaply because he used old car parts. He could sell his windmills for very little money. Lots of people bought them. Calley decided he did not need college to have a career—he had already found his career. He left school to make and sell his own windmills.

Andy Kruse was one of Calley's neighbors. Kruse lived on a cattle ranch that was very remote. It did not get electricity from a power company. Instead Kruse had to use a **generator** for all his power. This machine made power by burning diesel fuel. This cost a lot of

Andy Kruse, shown here, was so impressed with David Calley's windmill designs that the two men went into business together.

money. Kruse paid about three hundred dollars a month for the fuel. The machine also broke down a lot. It took up a lot of time for repairs.

A Mild Breeze Will Work

The wind blows at different speeds in different locations. Parts of the world get more wind than others. In the United States the strongest winds tend to be in California, Hawaii, Texas, and the Midwest. That makes these places ideal for making power from the wind. But home windmills do not need strong winds in order to make power. The blades of a home windmill can start turning in winds as low as 9 miles (14.5km) per hour. That is about as strong as a mild breeze that you can feel on your face.

Kruse decided there had to be a better way to get power on his ranch. He thought a windmill would be a good idea. He tried to build one himself. But he could not get it to work very well.

Then Kruse heard about Calley building small windmills in his father's garage. So Kruse decided to meet Calley and take a look at his idea. Once Kruse saw the type of windmill Calley had created, he said the two of them should go into business together.

The two men decided to name their new company Southwest Windpower. Calley became known as the "whiz-kid inventor." And Kruse became the marketing director for the company. Their company became so successful that soon they had more orders for their windmills than they could fill.

Early Challenges

At first Calley and Kruse built and tested their windmills in a garage that had no electricity. They already knew how to solve that problem, though. They built a windmill to power the garage. Calley kept using old car parts, such as **alternators** for generators. Instead of poles to attach the windmills to, they used cheaper water pipes from plumbing stores. Their first windmill was called the Windseeker. It was not very powerful. It only made about one-fifth as much power as other home windmills available at the time. But no one could beat Calley on price. His car-part and water-pipe windmills cost six

The first Windseeker windmill, pictured, was made from car parts and water pipes.

hundred dollars. Other windmills cost six thousand dollars.

Refining the Design

Calley and Kruse wanted to find ways to improve home windmills. They wanted to make them smaller and quieter. They wanted to design a windmill that would not need as much land as other windmills. That way more people could use one on their property. They also wanted to make windmills so affordable that most people could have and use one. Most of all, they wanted to find a way to make a windmill that did not need batteries to store the energy it produced.

Storing the electricity is one of the main challenges with home windmills. The power from a windmill must either

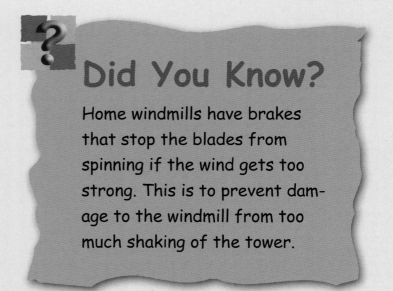

be used right away or be stored for later use. Early home windmills needed rows and rows of big batteries to store their power. This took up a lot of space. And many people did not like the sight of all those batteries on their property.

Many companies worked to solve the problem of storing power. They were trying to find ways to use fewer and smaller batteries. But Kruse and Calley wanted to design a windmill that did not even need a battery. They wanted to build a windmill that could connect to the wires that bring electricity directly into the home. This system is called the **power grid**. The wires run from the power plant to homes and other buildings. Hooking a home windmill up to the power grid would mean batteries would not be needed to store the power.

The Skystream

Kruse and Calley kept working to solve these challenges. They came up with a new model called the Skystream 3.7 in 2006. The Skystream went a long way toward solving some of the drawbacks of other windmills.

The Skystream could make power in low wind speeds. It starts working in winds as low as 9 miles (14.5km) per hour. At that rate, leaves on trees

The Skystream windmill is strong and lightweight, and it doesn't need a lot of space.

The Home Windmill Survives a Tornado

A home windmill owner awoke late one night to the howl of high winds. He quickly looked outside. He was amazed by what he saw. The tower of his windmill was snapping back and forth from the gusts of wind. He said, "The wind gusts were so harsh that it was actually rocking the tower back and forth like a screaming gorilla on a flag pole who just noticed a kid stole his banana." He thought the windmill would not last through the night. But in the morning, his windmill was still standing. It was not harmed by the storm. And because of the high winds, the windmill made a huge amount of electricity that night.

just begin to rustle. The Skystream reaches its full power in 20-mile-per-hour (32km per hour) winds. In winds of that strength, small trees will begin to sway. Because the Skystream works at lower wind speeds, it takes fewer turns per minute for the blades to make power than other models. This also makes the windmill quieter. The sound the spinning blades make is only about as loud as an air-conditioner or a refrigerator.

The Skystream is also small. It is about 34 feet (10m) tall. This is about as tall as a street light or telephone pole. Other windmills had to be as much as 100 feet (30.5m) tall. This is because they needed more wind in order to make the same amount of power as the Skystream. And the wind blows faster at higher **elevations**.

As with their other models, Calley and Kruse made the materials for the Skystream lightweight and **durable**. The

Skystream also needed much less land than other windmills. It will work on as little as 0.5 acre (0.2ha). Most home windmills need at least 1 acre (0.4ha) of land so that the wind is not blocked. But the Skystream needs less land because it works in lower wind speeds. That means it needs less clear area around it for the wind to blow freely.

Most important, the Skystream hooks up directly to the power grid. Any power that is not used right away can be sent to the power company. This means batteries are not needed to store power. Kruse and Calley had solved the problem of how to store the windmill's power without batteries. And this set the Skystream apart from other home windmills.

A Remote Control for Your Windmill?

Did you know that some windmills come with their own remote controls? People do not even have to go outside to start or stop the blades from spinning. They can just point the remote out the window and click a button.

The remote can be hooked up to a home's computer. Any problem with the windmill can be sent over the Internet to the manufacturer. They can then give advice on how to take care of the problem. It is as easy as changing the channel on the TV.

The Skystream Spreads to the World

The first Skystream was sold in October 2006. Within the first six months, the company had sold 450 of them. By the

The Skystream model makes energy near Mount Everest in Asia's Himalaya mountain range.

The Skystream requires far less land than other wind generators. Here, Skystreams easily fit on a small patch of beach in the Maldives.

end of 2007 they had sold 13,000. Southwest Windpower became the world's largest maker of home windmills. The Skystream could be found in 120 countries around the world.

Kruse explained the company's success in an interview. He said, "We had no real plan, just a dream. We made it work by keeping the overhead low and selling enough wind generators to pay the bills."

Chapter 3

How the Home Windmill Has Changed the World

In 1997 a couple in Illinois decided to build a new home. The land the Joneses bought for their home had open fields all around it. They knew this meant there would be a lot of wind. What they did not know was just how windy it would get. For ten years they listened to it howl past their house day and night. At times the wind would blow as fast as 40 miles (64km) per hour. At that speed, it is hard just to stand up straight when walking outside.

The Joneses decided to take advantage of their natural resources. They put a home windmill on their property in 2007. They started saving money right away. During the windiest part of the year, their power bills dropped from about ninety dollars per month to about ten dollars. Now the couple says the strong wind makes them happy because it means they are saving money.

Watching the Meter Spin

The Joneses are not the only ones who have saved money. Some windmill owners find they never have to pay the power company for power again. Others save up to 50 percent on their power. When the

Homeowners try out the clean power of the Skystream windmill. Excess power is stored in the local power grid.

wind blows and the blades spin, the windmill makes power for the home. When the wind does not blow, the home gets its power from the power company. But what happens when the wind is blowing so strong that the windmill makes more power than the home needs? In that case, the "extra" power is sent back to the power company. And in some places the power company pays the home windmill owner for this power.

Sometimes, home windmills work so well that their owners actually *make* money

Home of the Future

The "Home of the Future" was a display at the 1982 World's Fair. This was held in Knoxville, Tennessee. The house was shaped like a dome. It had solar panels on the roof. Beside it was a giant windmill that cost thirty thousand dollars. The windmill was much larger than the house needed. It could make twice as much power as the house could use. That is because it was actually designed to make power for many homes. In fact, the *New York Times* said it was "highly unlikely" that most homes of the future would actually have their own windmills. But this is starting to change. Now there are small windmills that cost less money and make enough power for single homes.

by using them. The windmill makes so much power that the **electric meter** spins backwards as power is being sent back to the power company. As one man in California told a newspaper reporter, "One of the top 10 pleasures in life is watching your electrical meter go backward."

Bringing Power to Remote Areas

About 2 billion people in the world do not have electric power. Many of them live in areas that are too remote for power lines to reach them. A good example is the ranch Andy Kruse lived on in Arizona. But in some parts of the world power lines simply do not exist. These people cannot refrigerate their food or have electric lights. People who live in these areas have to get by without electric power.

Home windmills can change that. Several companies, including Appropriate Energy, Inc., Bergey Windpower, and Southwest

Windmills in Antarctica can be seen against a darkening sky. Remote areas of the world rely on windmills for electric power.

Windpower, are making windmills that use a bank of batteries to store the extra power the windmills make. These batteries are smaller than ones used in the past. Today, fewer batteries are needed to store power than in the past. These windmills can be used in areas that are too far away to be connected to a power grid. Windmills help many people in these areas get power. They also make power for the local medical clinics. This is very important because many vaccines that prevent deadly diseases must be kept cold.

Home windmills are used in many rural places around the world. They pump water for nomadic herders in Mongolia. They make power for people doing research in Antarctica. And they are also used in the Arctic. The remote Raven Skyway camp is in Greenland, just above the Arctic Circle. The camp is powered by a windmill. Pilots use the skyway at the camp to practice landing airplanes on snow and ice. The site is also used for survival training.

Home windmills also help make power on remote Native American reservations in the United States. One example is the

Did You Know?

In the United States, 180,000 homes are completely off-grid. These homes get part or all of their power from home windmills. The rest comes from other alternative sources such as solar panels.

Navajo Nation in the Southwest. Some areas there still do not get power from the grid. So they installed two hundred windmills to help make power.

Wind Power Around the World

Windmills have been put up all over the world. In fact, windmills are at work in urban areas as well as rural areas. Windmills make power for street lights in Japan. And in Kyoto, Japan, home windmills provide power for schools. In fact, many of the city's schools have put up windmills. The schools use the power from their windmills in different ways. Some schools use

Japanese schoolchildren watch the installation of a windmill in Kyoto, where windmills often provide power for schools.

the windmills to pump water. Others use them to power the school's **public address system**. Still others use them to power their security alarms.

In 2007 the city of Berkeley, California also installed a home windmill on a city

Windmills Can Pay for Themselves

The price of home windmills varies. Today's home windmills cost between ten thousand and thirteen thousand dollars. That is a lot more money than Calley's original home windmill, but the new models are bigger and produce a lot more power. The savings come over time. Home windmills allow people to save money on their power bills. They can also earn money for any power the windmill makes that they do not use. It takes about twelve years for most home windmills to pay for themselves, although it can take longer.

How long it takes a windmill to pay for itself depends mainly on the windmill's cost, and the wind speed and cost of electricity in a given area. In windier areas, a home windmill can make more power. That means it will pay for itself more quickly. In places where the power costs more, the windmill will also pay for itself more quickly.

building. This windmill sits on top of the Shorebird Nature Center. The windmill produces between 60 and 80 percent of the building's electricity.

Going Green

Many people around the world want to "go green." They want to use energy that does not pollute the air or the planet. Home windmills are helping them to do this.

Home windmills used to be used mainly in rural areas that were far away from the power company. But that has started to change. Windmill companies are making home windmills that do not need batteries. Now people can "plug and play" their windmills. This means they can connect the windmill directly to the home's power supply. They no longer need big, expensive batteries to store the power. This makes it much easier for them to go green.

This has led to a new trend in urban areas. Now entire neighborhoods can go green. The Three Rivers community in Oregon is a good example. Everyone there lives off the grid. This means they do not get their power from a utility company. Instead, they make all their own power. They do this with the help of home windmills.

The people who live in the 250 homes in Three Rivers are happy to be living green. One man who lives there told a reporter, "Ninety percent of the people here, if (outside) power were offered to them, they'd turn it down." He explained an added benefit to living off the grid: "There are no power outages here."

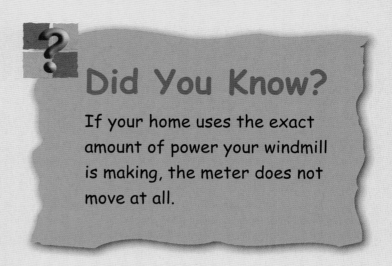

Did You Know?

If your home uses the exact amount of power your windmill is making, the meter does not move at all.

Building a Better World

The Skystream has been around for a short time, but it is already starting to help people around the world. And the company is already winning awards for its new windmill.

The first award came before the new windmill was even ready to be sold to the public. The company won an award for

A groundbreaking housing development near Chorley, England includes energy efficient windmills and solar panels on new homes.

its design. Then the new windmill was given two more awards. One was given by *Time* magazine. The other was given by *Popular Science*. Both awards were for technology that is a big step forward from what already exists.

David Calley and Andy Kruse are happy that their company is doing well. They are glad that people like the idea of home windmills. But being successful is not just about winning awards and making money. From the start Calley and Kruse had a main goal in mind. The major reason they wanted to make windmills was to bring power to people in remote areas. They wanted to help improve people's lives.

What Would You Do with Fifty Dollars?

A home windmill can supply from 35 to 70 percent of a home's power. That means windmill owners can save a lot of money. The average home can save six hundred dollars or more a year with a windmill. That is a savings of fifty dollars each month.

Chapter 4

What's Next for Home Windmills?

Today, people must buy home windmills directly from the company that makes them. But someday stores in your neighborhood may carry home windmills. Then people can buy a windmill as easily as a new washing machine. Many people hope to see every home in the world have its own windmill someday.

Surprisingly though, home windmills are not just for homes. They can be used aboard ships, too. Modern sailboats have lots of high-tech equipment that requires power. For instance, an onboard computer may help with navigation. Because the wind is already strong enough to blow the sails, the wind can easily power a small windmill.

Small windmills can also be used for sites that relay TV, radio, telephone, and Internet signals. Often these sites are located

Sailboats with special tools for navigation use small windmills for their electrical power needs.

on tall towers in very remote areas. They can be found on mountaintops or at sea. Many of these sites are powered by generators that run on gas. Small windmills let the site use less power from the generator.

A good example of this is a site on Big Mountain in Alaska. This site relays both microwave and cell phone signals. The site can be reached only by helicopter. This makes fuel for the generator very costly. But two small windmills provide most of the power for the site. This helps save money. It also helps prevent air pollution.

People have even found a use for small windmills below the ground. Windmills help protect metal pipes that are underground or in water. This includes oil and natural gas pipelines. The moisture can eat away at these pipes. But sending a low-voltage electric current through the pipes can stop this damage. Home windmills provide just the right amount of electric current for this task. They are used to protect pipes around the world.

One more way home windmills are used is to make power at monitoring sites around the world. These sites keep track

A Regular Home Appliance

Andy Kruse and David Calley have high hopes for windmills. They would like to see windmills become just like any other machine in the home. They believe the day will come when home windmills will be as common as stoves and refrigerators.

Your Own Personal Windmill?

Someday you may be able to walk around with your own personal windmill folded into a canvas bag. The Wing Personal Windmill was designed by two men in Croatia. Their idea was to make a windmill that you can carry around with you. It folds up like a lawn chair to make it easy to carry. And it makes just enough power for things like charging your cell phone or running your laptop. You could even take it camping with you and use it to power a lamp when it gets dark outside.

of facts about the oceans, the weather, and animal life, among other things. Some of these sites are run by groups such as Greenpeace and NASA. Others are run by governments or private companies.

One example of monitoring sites that use wind power is found in the Andes Mountains. An oil pipeline there runs about 750 miles (1,200km) from Argentina to Chile. Thirteen sites keep track of conditions along the pipeline. Five of these sites use power from the grid. But at eight of these sites there is no other power. These sites use windmills to help create the power on-site. They also use **solar panels**.

Windmills and Solar Panels

Windmills are often used along with solar panels to make clean power. Using these two methods together makes sense. That is because the sun does not always shine. And the wind does not always blow. By having a windmill and solar panels, people can make the most of both.

A home in France uses the dual power sources of wind power and solar panels for its needs.

tain. People who get hurt can go there for help. This clinic gets all its power by using a windmill combined with solar panels.

Did You Know?

Putting windmills higher up where the wind is stronger means they can make more power. One company is working on a windmill that will "float." This windmill will be inside a stationary blimp that is held up by helium. It will be able to make up to twice as much power as a windmill at ground level.

An example of this is found in Nepal. Each year many people climb Mount Everest. It is the tallest mountain in the world. It is also very remote. There are no electric lines on Mount Everest. And there are no hospitals. But there is a clinic on the moun-

Rooftop Windmills

Some people think about putting a wind-mill on the roofs of houses. That way, homes in the city could use them. And even people without a big backyard could use them. But there is a problem with this idea. The spinning blades of a windmill make the pole vibrate. The pole can shake enough to cause damage to the roof.

Several companies are working on ways to improve rooftop windmills. One of these is Quiet Revolution. This company in England has come up with a new design. Its rooftop windmill has three S-shaped blades. It is not very tall—only 16 feet (5m). And it barely vibrates when the blades spin. A new pub that opened in England in September 2007 was the first to install one of these rooftop windmills.

The owner bought the windmill to save money on his bills. He expects to use 50 percent less energy at the pub.

A wind turbine sits atop a Dutch roof. As technology improves, rooftop windmills may become more common.

Did You Know?

Several companies are working on windmills that will "fly." The spinning blades keep the windmills afloat. These windmills will be 3 to 6 miles (4.8 to 9.7km) high, where the winds are extremely strong. The power gets back down to the earth through aluminum cables that are attached to the windmill and keep it from flying away.

Windmills on Mars?

One day windmills may be used on Mars. NASA is considering using wind-mills developed for use at the South Pole and in Alaska to make power for future bases on Mars. The planet is famous for its dust storms that can last for weeks at a time. During the dust storms Mars is in darkness. But windmills would be able to make power during these storms, since the wind is blowing. That means bases on

No Location Too Remote

Home windmills are used to make power for everything from sailboats to radar sites for airplanes. But the vice president of Southwest Windpower found a unique place for a windmill. One of his friends has a home windmill in a tree house.

Mars would have the power to light up the darkest days.

And Now . . . Cars!

Windmills truly are everywhere. But David Calley's interest in machines goes beyond windmills. He has always loved cars. He says that as soon as windmills become as common in homes as any other machine, he would like to move on to cars.

Calley has been doing experiments on his own **hybrid** car. This small car uses electric power and pedal power. It is about the size of a Vespa scooter. It gets up to 30 percent of its energy from the driver pedaling. Calley thinks his car will help with two problems people face. He says, "One, our vehicles are far, far, far too big and two, we don't get enough exercise."

In Tokyo, Japan, a woman recharges an electric car. Many kinds of hybrid cars are being developed to keep up with consumer demand.

With a car like this, people could get their exercise while they run errands. They could also save money on gas. And they would be helping the planet by reducing the pollution in the air.

Currently, Calley drives an electric car—and he charges the car's battery with a home windmill.

One Windmill at a Time

Wind energy will never be able to provide 100 percent of the power people use. That is because the wind does not always blow. And it does not blow at the same rate all the time or in all parts of the world. But windmills can supply power to millions of homes in the United States. And in doing so, home windmills can help reduce air pollution and maybe even slow the advance of global warming. Someone long ago came up with the idea of harnessing the power of the wind for energy, and modern home windmills are making that great idea a reality for people around the globe.

A steel forest of windmill turbines lines Interstate 10 near Palm Springs, California.

Glossary

alternators: Devices in cars that change the energy of the running motor into electricity.

carbon dioxide: A gas that occurs naturally in the air and helps to hold the earth's heat in.

durable: Made to last a long time.

electric meter: A meter that measures electrical use in a home or building.

elevations: The height of objects, measured from the earth's surface or sea level.

fossil fuels: Fuels that come from the remains of plants and animals that died millions of years ago.

generator: A machine that changes mechanical energy into electricity.

global warming: A gradual rise in global temperatures. It is caused by too much carbon dioxide and other gases that trap the sun's heat in the earth's atmosphere.

hybrid: A machine such as a car that runs partly on gas and partly on electricity.

hydroelectric dams: Dams that use the movement of flowing water to make electricity.

mill: To grind or chop something such as grains or wood.

power grid: The system of wires that carries power from the power plant to homes and other buildings.

public address system: A system that

uses a microphone and several loud-speakers to carry a person's voice throughout a building such as a school.

solar panels: Panels that gather sunlight and change it into electricity.

turbines: Devices that make power by using the movement of air, steam, or water to turn the blades of a wheel. Windmills that are used to make electricity are called turbines.

For More Information

Web Sites

The Energy Story—Chapter 16: Wind Energy, Energy Quest (www.energy quest.ca.gov/story/chapter16.html). This Web site uses kid-friendly language to explain all about how wind turbines work.

Skystream Energy (http://www.skystream energy.com). This Web site gives a detailed explanation of how the Skystream 3.7 home wind generator works.

Wind Energy—Energy from Moving Air, Energy Kid's Page (www.eia.doe. gov/kids/energyfacts/sources/renewable/ wind.html). This section of the U.S. Department of Energy's Kid's Page gives lots of information about wind energy, including its history, types of wind machines, wind power plants, the impact of wind turbines on the environment, and links to other helpful Web sites.

Wind with Miller (www.windpower.org/ en/kids/index.htm). Using kid-friendly language, this Web site offers a "crash course" in the basics of wind energy. There are also many activities for kids, including making a wind sock, a kite, and a small wind turbine.

Index

About the Author

Cherese Cartlidge is a freelance writer and editor. Her fascination with windmills started in childhood, when her mother used to sketch and paint pictures of windmills.

Cartlidge has written several books for young people. She is a former teacher who loves being around children so much that she has two of her very own, Thomas and Liv. When she is not writing or editing, she loves to take long walks in the park with her ninety-six-pound rottweiler puppy.